Chapter 1: The Power o Mind

Welcome to the captivating journey of self-discovery and personal transformation. In the epic narrative of life, the starring role belongs to none other than the state of our minds. Every thought, every belief, carefully crafted by both internal convictions and external influences, weaves the tapestry of our perception, dictating the choices that carve our destiny. The lens through which we observe reality, be it one of boundless optimism or unwavering pessimism, wields an awe-inspiring influence over our day-to-day experiences and the grand tapestry of our lives.

This inaugural chapter delves deep into the resounding impact of our mental fortitude on the very essence of our existence. It promises not just an exploration but a guiding light, offering pragmatic insights and lived experiences to empower you in nurturing an unshakable positive mindset while expertly navigating the labyrinth of anxiety and the entanglement of phobias.

Nurturing the Seed of Positivity

At the heart of our journey lies a profound understanding: our state of mind, that compass through life's labyrinth, holds the power to shape our experiences in every conceivable manner. Let us imagine two individuals confronted by an identical, challenging juncture. One, illuminated by the beacon of a positive mindset, perceives it as a golden opportunity for growth and enlightenment, while the other, ensnared in the web of negativity, dreads it as an impassable fortress. These perspectives, dichotomous as they seem, draw their lifeblood from the realms of their mental states.

Techniques of Transformation

Crafting a radiant and unwavering positive mindset is a voyage that unfurls over time. Yet, the arsenal at your disposal is both potent and unerring, the embodiment of your power to shape your mental world. Embrace these powerful tools as your own:

Mindfulness: Gaze deeply into the mirror of your thoughts and emotions. Recognize those lurking shadows of negativity, confront them, and replace them with the vibrant hues of constructive thinking.

Gratitude: Take a moment to revel in the exquisite beauty of the present. Instead of lamenting what is absent, bathe in the luminous glow of your current blessings. This practice breeds contentment and begets happiness.

Affirmations: Speak to yourself, for your words can mold your reality. Convey to your soul that you are capable, confident, and resolute. In time, these affirmations will breathe life into your self-fulfilling prophecies.

The Company of Inspiration: Seek out the companionship of positivity. Whether through the pages of wisdom-laden books, the symphonies of motivational podcasts, or the camaraderie of uplifting friends, immerse yourself in a sea of inspiration and encouragement.

Harnessing the Winds of Anxiety and Phobia

Anxiety and phobias, akin to tempests within, can wreak havoc on your life's grand voyage. Yet, remember this, you possess the helm to steer your ship through the stormy seas of your own thoughts and emotions.

Relaxation Techniques: Embrace the serenity offered by relaxation methods. Employ deep breathing, meditation, or the tranquil art of progressive muscle relaxation to quell the tumultuous storms of anxiety that rage within.

Cognitive-Behavioral Mastery: Challenge the shackles of negative thought patterns that feed the flames of your anxiety. Replace them with rational and uplifting alternatives that pave the way for tranquility.

A Gradual Conquest: If a phobia casts its shadow over your life, take the helm and steer toward the sunrise of courage. Gradually expose yourself to the feared object or situation while nurturing your spirit with the soothing balm of positive affirmations and vivid visualizations. Your transformation into an indomitable force begins one step at a time.

This is just the prologue of your adventure. As you turn the pages of this book, the chapters that follow promise profound revelations, boundless wisdom, and the unwavering belief that you possess the power to write your own destiny. Welcome to a life defined by resilience, positivity, and the unyielding pursuit of greatness. Your journey starts now.

Chapter 2: Thriving in the Workplace: A Positive Approach

In the fast-paced world of the modern workplace, success is not solely determined by skill and knowledge. A positive perspective on your career can be a game-changer, influencing your job satisfaction, productivity, and overall professional growth. This chapter delves into strategies to embrace positivity in your career, manage time and stress effectively, boost self-esteem and confidence, and cultivate a success-oriented mindset with the help of practical tips and real-life examples.

Tip 1: Embracing Positivity in Your Career

Your attitude toward your career profoundly impacts your performance and job satisfaction. Embracing a positive outlook in the workplace can transform your daily experiences and long-term prospects.

Consider two coworkers faced with the same challenging project. One views it as an opportunity to learn and grow, while the other sees it as an overwhelming burden. The first employee approaches the project with enthusiasm, leading to a sense of accomplishment, increased competence, and potentially, recognition and career advancement. The second employee's negative attitude can lead to stress, lower job performance, and even missed opportunities for growth.

Tip 2: Effective Time and Stress Management

Time management and stress management are essential skills in any career. A positive perspective can greatly enhance your ability to excel in these areas.

a. Prioritization: Focus on high-impact tasks that align with your goals and values. Avoid the urge to engage in unproductive activities that drain your time and energy.

Imagine you're a project manager with multiple deadlines. Instead of constantly firefighting minor issues, prioritize tasks, allocate resources efficiently, and maintain a clear vision of the project's objectives. This positive approach reduces stress and enhances your reputation for effective leadership.

b. Time Blocking: Allocate specific time blocks for tasks, minimizing distractions and multitasking. This approach improves concentration and productivity.

For example, if you're a writer, designate a block of time each day for writing without interruptions. This positive habit enhances your writing quality and output.

c. Stress Management: A positive mindset can help you navigate stressful situations by viewing them as opportunities for personal growth rather than insurmountable challenges.

For example, when facing a tight deadline, view it as a chance to showcase your abilities, rather than an anxiety-inducing ordeal. A positive outlook can lead to better performance and a sense of accomplishment.

Tip 3: Building Self-Esteem and Confidence at Work

Your self-esteem and confidence play a pivotal role in your career. By cultivating a positive self-image, you can boost your professional growth and potential.

a. Self-Reflection: Take time to reflect on your achievements and strengths. Celebrate your successes, no matter how small they may seem.

For example, after a successful presentation at a business meeting, take a moment to recognize your accomplishments and pat yourself on the back. This self-affirmation builds confidence and self-esteem.

b. Continuous Learning: Embrace a growth mindset, always seeking opportunities for learning and improvement. Acknowledge that setbacks are part of the journey.

For example, if you receive constructive feedback from a supervisor, see it as a chance for growth rather than criticism. Embrace the feedback with a positive attitude and a commitment to improving your skills.

Tip 4: Cultivating a Success-Oriented Mindset

Success in your career often hinges on your mindset. A success-oriented perspective can propel you forward by fostering resilience, determination, and an unwavering commitment to your goals.

a. Goal Setting: Set clear, achievable goals for your career. A positive mindset can help you stay focused and committed to your objectives.

As a sales representative, set monthly targets for revenue. With a success-oriented mindset, you'll be more likely to push through challenges, explore new strategies, and achieve your sales goals.

b. Visualization: Envision your success. Visualization can boost your confidence and motivation, making your career aspirations more attainable.

If you're an athlete, visualize yourself crossing the finish line first or scoring a crucial point. This positive mental rehearsal can translate into better performance on the field.

Approaching your career with a positive perspective can be a transformative force. Embracing positivity, mastering time and stress management, building self-esteem and confidence, and cultivating a success-oriented mindset are not just strategies for professional growth but keys to unlocking your full potential. By incorporating these tips and learning from real-life examples, you can build a rewarding and successful career that aligns with your aspirations and values.

Chapter 3: Cultivating a Positive Home Environment

In the chaotic and demanding world outside, the home should be a sanctuary of peace, support, and love. Nurturing a positive atmosphere within your home not only benefits you but also influences the well-being of your family members. This chapter explores strategies to embrace positivity in the family setting, integrating the lessons of effective career mindset, time management, stress management, self-esteem, and success-oriented thinking into the heart of your home.

Tip 1: Creating a Positive Family Culture

Just as a positive attitude can transform your career, it can create a more harmonious family environment. Cultivating positivity at home starts with setting a constructive tone for interactions, mutual respect, and communication.

Instead of dwelling on disagreements, family members can focus on shared goals and values. For instance, if you're a parent, fostering a sense of unity among your children by emphasizing kindness, empathy, and respect can create a more positive atmosphere at home.

Tip 2: Effective Time Management in Family Life

Balancing work, personal life, and family can be a juggling act. Effective time management at home ensures that family members have time for meaningful interactions, relaxation, and shared experiences.

a. Scheduling Family Time: Dedicate specific times for family activities, such as dinner together, game nights, or outings. This fosters a sense of togetherness and provides quality time for bonding.

If you're a working parent, create a family calendar that includes dedicated family time. This proactive approach ensures that family time is prioritized alongside work commitments.

b. Time for Self-Care: Encourage every family member to have time for self-care activities that recharge their spirits, reduce stress, and promote well-being.

Promote a positive home environment by valuing each family member's need for self-care. This could mean respecting your teenager's space and time for hobbies or allowing your spouse to relax after a demanding workday.

Tip 3: Building Self-Esteem and Confidence in Family Relationships

Self-esteem and confidence are not limited to the workplace; they are essential for nurturing healthy family relationships. Encouraging your loved ones to have a positive self-image and high self-worth can strengthen your family bonds.

a. Encouragement and Affirmation: Offer encouragement and affirmations to family members. Compliments and positive feedback can boost their self-esteem and confidence.

If you're a parent, celebrate your child's achievements, both big and small. Encouraging their efforts and acknowledging their growth can enhance their self-esteem.

b. Active Listening: Listening to one another without judgment or criticism is crucial for building trust and confidence within the family.

In a marital relationship, active listening ensures that both partners feel heard and valued. This fosters open communication and a supportive, loving atmosphere.

Tip 4: Cultivating a Success-Oriented Mindset at Home

Just as a success-oriented mindset can drive career growth, it can also inspire achievement and resilience within the family setting.

a. Setting Family Goals: Establish goals and ambitions as a family unit. These may encompass educational achievements, personal growth, or community involvement.

Set a goal of volunteering as a family in local charities. This not only teaches your children the value of giving back but also nurtures a success-oriented mindset built on empathy and community involvement.

b. Teaching Resilience: Resilience is a key component of a success-oriented mindset. Encourage family members to view setbacks as opportunities for growth.

If a family member faces a disappointment, discuss it openly as a learning experience. Help them recognize that resilience and the ability to adapt are valuable life skills.

Your home should be a place where positivity thrives, and family members find support and love. By applying the principles of effective career mindset, time management, stress management, self-esteem, and success-oriented thinking to your family life, you can create a more nurturing and harmonious home environment. Through these tips and real-life examples, you'll find that cultivating a positive home life enriches the well-being of each family member and strengthens the bonds of love and support that hold your family together.

Chapter 4: Building Stronger Relationships

In the intricate tapestry of human existence, relationships are the threads that connect us. Whether romantic, familial, or platonic, these connections form the heart of our lives. This chapter explores strategies to build stronger relationships, incorporating the lessons of positive thinking, effective communication, stress management, and self-esteem maintenance.

Tip 1: Positive Thinking in Romantic Relationships

In the realm of love, positive thinking is a powerful tool that can shape the quality and longevity of romantic relationships. Embracing positivity can infuse your partnership with joy, resilience, and mutual support.

a. Fostering Gratitude: Express appreciation and gratitude for your partner regularly. Focus on their qualities and the positive aspects of your relationship.

Instead of taking your partner for granted, express gratitude for their thoughtfulness, support, or affection. This simple act can strengthen the bond of love.

b. Seeing Challenges as Opportunities: Positive thinking allows you to view relationship challenges as opportunities for growth rather than insurmountable problems.

If you and your partner face a disagreement, approach it as a chance to better understand each other's perspectives. With a positive mindset, you can navigate the conflict constructively.

Tip 2: Communication and Conflict Resolution from a Positive Perspective

Effective communication and conflict resolution are essential components of any healthy relationship. A positive perspective can enhance your ability to convey your feelings, listen actively, and resolve disputes constructively.

a. Active Listening: Truly listening to your partner fosters a positive connection. Show empathy and validate their feelings.

When your partner shares their concerns or joys, listen attentively and respond with empathy. Active listening builds trust and mutual understanding.

b. Use "I" Statements: Instead of blaming or criticizing, express your feelings using "I" statements, which take responsibility for your emotions.

Instead of saying, "You never listen to me," say, "I feel unheard when we argue, and it upsets me." This approach opens a dialogue and encourages empathy.

c. Resolution, Not Winning: Approach conflicts with the intention of finding a solution together, not to "win" the argument.

If you and your partner disagree about household responsibilities, approach the discussion with a focus on finding a compromise that works for both of you.

Tip 3: Managing Stress within a Partnership

Stress is an inevitable part of life, and it can impact relationships. A positive perspective on stress can help you and your partner cope and maintain a strong connection.

a. Shared Coping Strategies: Develop shared strategies for managing stress as a couple, such as relaxation techniques, exercise, or mindful activities.

If both partners are feeling stressed, going for a calming walk together or practicing deep breathing exercises can help reduce tension and promote a positive atmosphere.

b. Give Space When Needed: Recognize that sometimes individuals need space to manage stress. Respect your partner's need for solitude when it arises.

If one partner has a particularly stressful day, giving them some alone time to unwind can prevent unnecessary conflicts and maintain a positive atmosphere.

Tip 4: Maintaining Self-Esteem in Love

Self-esteem is a cornerstone of any healthy relationship. A positive perspective on self-esteem allows you and your partner to love and support each other while nurturing personal growth.

a. Mutual Support: Encourage and support each other's self-esteem. Celebrate each other's achievements and provide reassurance.

If your partner achieves a personal milestone, celebrate their success, and express pride in their accomplishments. This support boosts their self-esteem.

b. Acceptance and Respect: A positive relationship thrives on acceptance and respect for each other's individuality.

Accept your partner for who they are, recognizing that their quirks and differences are what make them unique. Respect their individual choices and values.

Building stronger relationships requires a positive perspective that nurtures love, trust, and mutual growth. By incorporating positive thinking, effective communication, stress management, and self-esteem maintenance into your relationships, you can create bonds that are not only enduring but also filled with love, understanding, and personal support. Through these tips and real-life examples, you'll discover that a positive approach to relationships enriches both your life and the lives of those you cherish.

Chapter 5: The Friendships That Uplift

Friendships are like a garden where positivity can bloom. The relationships we choose to cultivate can have a profound impact on our well-being and outlook on life. In this chapter, we'll explore how to build and maintain uplifting friendships by choosing friends who promote positivity, navigating conflicts with a positive outlook, reducing social anxiety and fear of rejection, and ultimately finding joy in your social connections.

Tip 1: Choosing Friends Who Promote Positivity

The first step in nurturing uplifting friendships is to carefully select those who promote positivity in your life. Your friends should be a source of support, encouragement, and inspiration.

a. Common Values and Goals: Seek friends who share your values and life goals. Aligning with like-minded individuals can create a harmonious and positive friendship.

If you're passionate about volunteering and community service, connecting with friends who also value social responsibility can lead to meaningful and positive friendships.

b. Mutual Respect and Empathy: A positive friendship thrives on mutual respect and empathy. Your friends should respect your boundaries, feelings, and choices.

If you communicate your need for some alone time, a supportive friend will understand and respect your boundaries, enhancing the positive nature of your friendship.

Tip 2: Navigating Friendship Conflicts with a Positive Outlook

Friendship conflicts are a natural part of any relationship, but they don't have to be destructive. Navigating them with a positive perspective can strengthen your friendships.

a. Open and Honest Communication: Address conflicts with open and honest communication. Approach disagreements as opportunities for understanding and growth, not as battles to win.

If a friend cancel plan last-minute and you feel hurt, express your feelings calmly and openly. By communicating your emotions positively, you can work together to find a resolution.

b. Forgiveness and Letting Go: Learning to forgive and let go of grudges is a crucial aspect of positive conflict resolution.

If a friend apologizes for an oversight, accept the apology and move forward with a positive attitude. Holding onto past grievances can harm your friendship and your own well-being.

Tip 3: Reducing Social Anxiety and Fear of Rejection

Social anxiety and the fear of rejection can hinder your ability to form and maintain friendships. Reducing these fears through positive thinking is essential.

a. Self-Confidence and Self-Esteem: Building self-confidence and self-esteem can help reduce social anxiety and fear of rejection. Believe in your worth as a friend.

If you're hesitant to attend a social event because of social anxiety, remind yourself of your qualities and the positive aspects you bring to any friendship. Embrace your self-worth.

b. Positive Self-Talk: Replace negative self-talk with positive affirmations that reinforce your social competence and self-worth.

Instead of telling yourself, "I'll embarrass myself," affirm, "I am a great friend, and people enjoy my company." This shift in thinking can reduce social anxiety.

Tip 4: Finding Joy in Your Social Connections

Ultimately, the goal of nurturing uplifting friendships is to find joy and fulfillment in your social connections.

a. Shared Experiences: Create joy in your friendships by sharing meaningful experiences and creating positive memories.

Plan outings, adventures, or simple gatherings with friends to create shared experiences that bring joy and strengthen your bond.

b. Laughter and Positivity: Infuse humor and positivity into your friendships. Laughter is a powerful tool for building connections and spreading joy.

Share jokes, funny stories, or watch a comedy show with your friends. Laughter can be a wonderful source of happiness in your friendships.

Uplifting friendships can bring immeasurable joy and support into your life. By choosing friends who promote positivity, navigating conflicts with a positive outlook, reducing social anxiety and fear of rejection, and finding joy in your social connections, you can create a circle of friends who inspire and uplift you. Through these tips and real-life examples, you'll discover that nurturing positive friendships not only enhances your well-being but also enriches the lives of those who share in your positive journey.

Chapter 6: Empowering Self-Worth: Mastering Self-Esteem

Self-esteem is the cornerstone of personal growth and well-being. The way we view ourselves influences every aspect of our lives, from our relationships to our career success. In this chapter, we will explore the role of self-esteem in personal development, uncover techniques for boosting self-worth and self-confidence, learn how to manage self-doubt and negative self-talk, and celebrate the unique qualities that make each individual extraordinary.

Understanding the Role of Self-Esteem in Personal Growth

Self-esteem is the foundation upon which personal growth is built. It shapes the decisions we make, the relationships we engage in, and the goals we pursue.

Imagine a person with low self-esteem who doubts their abilities and self-worth. They may shy away from challenges, avoid opportunities for growth, and settle for less than they deserve. In contrast, an individual with healthy self-esteem believes in their capabilities and values themselves. They are more likely to embrace opportunities, seek personal growth, and pursue their aspirations.

Techniques for Boosting Self-Worth and Self-Confidence

Positive Affirmations: Use positive affirmations to rewire your thought patterns. Repeat statements that reinforce your self-worth and confidence.

Daily affirmations like "I am capable and worthy" can gradually boost self-esteem and self-confidence.

Set Achievable Goals: Establish small, achievable goals and celebrate your successes. Each accomplishment contributes to your sense of self-worth.

If you set a goal to exercise regularly, celebrate each workout as a win. Recognize your commitment and dedication.

Practice Self-Compassion: Be kind to yourself, especially when you make mistakes or face setbacks. Treat yourself as you would treat a dear friend.

Instead of criticizing yourself for an error at work, offer self-compassion by acknowledging that everyone makes mistakes and focusing on what you've learned from the experience.

Managing Self-Doubt and Negative Self-Talk

Self-doubt and negative self-talk are common challenges, but they can be managed with awareness and positive strategies.

Challenge Negative Thoughts: When negative self-talk arises, challenge it. Ask yourself if there's evidence to support those negative beliefs.

If you think, "I'm not smart enough for this job," challenge that thought by reflecting on your qualifications and achievements.

Practice Mindfulness: Engage in mindfulness practices to become aware of your thoughts without judgment. This awareness can help you detach from negative self-talk.

During meditation, observe negative thoughts without reacting to them emotionally. This practice can reduce the impact of self-doubt.

Surround Yourself with Positivity: Choose to be around people who uplift and support you. Positive influences can counteract negative self-talk.

Seek out friends and mentors who believe in your capabilities and remind you of your strengths.

Celebrating Your Uniqueness

Each person possesses a unique blend of qualities, experiences, and perspectives that make them special. Celebrating your uniqueness is a powerful way to boost self-esteem and appreciate your worth.

Identify Your Strengths: Recognize your strengths and talents, no matter how small they may seem. They contribute to your uniqueness.

If you have a talent for making people laugh, celebrate your ability to spread joy and positivity.

Embrace Your Flaws: Your flaws and imperfections are part of what makes you unique. Embrace them as part of your individuality.

If you're an introvert, celebrate your ability to listen and reflect deeply, which can be a valuable trait in certain situations.

Pursue Your Passions: Engage in activities and passions that light your inner fire. Pursuing what you love can boost self-esteem and remind you of your uniqueness.

If you're passionate about painting, immerse yourself in your art. The act of creating can be a powerful affirmation of your unique creativity.

Mastering self-esteem is the key to personal growth, happiness, and success. By understanding its role in personal development, implementing techniques to boost self-worth and self-confidence, managing self-doubt and negative self-talk, and celebrating your uniqueness, you can build a foundation of self-esteem that empowers you to pursue your dreams, embrace your individuality, and thrive in all aspects of your life. Through these tips and real-life examples, you'll discover that self-esteem is not only a source of personal strength but also the driving force behind your unique potential.

Chapter 7: Thriving Through Adversity: Stress Management and Resilience

Life is a journey filled with challenges and uncertainties. How we cope with stress and build resilience in the face of adversity can profoundly impact our well-being and overall success. In this chapter, we will explore strategies for coping with stress through positive thinking, building emotional resilience, reducing the impact of negative external factors, and embracing change and uncertainty with positivity.

Coping with Stress through Positive Thinking

Stress is an inevitable part of life, but our perspective on it can make a significant difference. Positive thinking can be a powerful tool for managing and even thriving in the face of stress.

Reframing Challenges: Positive thinking involves reframing challenges as opportunities for growth. By viewing stressors as a chance to learn and improve, you can reduce their impact on your well-being.

If you face a tight deadline at work, consider it an opportunity to showcase your skills and determination rather than a source of stress.

Mindfulness and Relaxation: Mindfulness practices, such as meditation and deep breathing, can calm the mind and reduce stress. These techniques promote a positive outlook by allowing you to stay present in the moment.

Taking a few moments each day to practice deep breathing or meditation can alleviate stress and help you maintain a positive perspective.

Building Emotional Resilience

Emotional resilience is the ability to bounce back from adversity and maintain mental well-being. It can be cultivated through various strategies.

Acceptance of Emotions: Emotional resilience involves accepting and processing your emotions, even the negative ones. This self-awareness allows you to address them and move forward.

If you experience grief after a loss, acknowledging and processing your emotions is an important step in building emotional resilience.

Seeking Support: Reach out to friends, family, or a therapist for emotional support when facing adversity. Opening up and seeking help is a sign of emotional strength.

If you're going through a difficult time, confiding in a trusted friend or therapist can provide the emotional support needed to build resilience.

Reducing the Impact of Negative External Factors

Negative external factors, such as toxic relationships or a stressful work environment, can significantly contribute to stress. It's crucial to reduce their impact on your well-being.

Setting Boundaries: Establish clear boundaries with toxic individuals or situations. This allows you to protect your mental and emotional well-being.

If a friendship is consistently draining and negative, set boundaries or reconsider the relationship's place in your life.

Seeking a Supportive Environment: Surround yourself with a supportive and nurturing environment that fosters positivity and personal growth.

If your workplace is causing excessive stress, consider exploring other job opportunities or seeking a supportive work environment.

Embracing Change and Uncertainty with Positivity

Change and uncertainty are constants in life. Embracing them with a positive outlook can help you navigate through these challenges.

Adapting to Change: Approach change as an opportunity for growth and learning. A positive outlook allows you to adapt more effectively.

If you experience a change in your personal life, such as relocating to a new city, see it as a chance for new experiences and personal growth.

Embracing Uncertainty: Uncertainty can be unsettling, but it also offers the potential for adventure and surprise. Embrace it with curiosity and positivity.

When facing uncertain times, approach them with a mindset of curiosity and an openness to new possibilities.

Stress management and resilience are essential skills for thriving through adversity. By coping with stress through positive thinking, building emotional resilience, reducing the impact of negative external factors, and embracing change and uncertainty with positivity, you can navigate life's challenges with grace and determination. These strategies, accompanied by real-life examples, illustrate that adversity can be a source of growth and personal transformation when faced with a positive mindset.

Chapter 8: Courage Beyond Fear: Overcoming Anxieties and Phobias

Anxieties and phobias can be formidable barriers on the path to personal growth and well-being. This chapter delves into strategies for confronting and conquering fears, the pivotal role of positivity in managing anxiety disorders, the importance of seeking professional help when needed, and the transformative power of turning fear into an opportunity for personal growth.

Strategies for Confronting and Conquering Fears

Exposure Therapy: Gradual exposure to the feared object or situation can help desensitize the anxiety response. Start with less intimidating scenarios and progressively work your way up.

If you have a fear of flying, you might begin by researching flight safety, then visiting an airport, and ultimately taking a short flight.

Cognitive Restructuring: Identify and challenge the negative thought patterns that fuel anxieties and phobias. Replace them with more rational and positive alternatives.

If you have a fear of public speaking, you can reframe negative thoughts like "I'll embarrass myself" with "I have prepared well, and I can deliver a great presentation."

The Role of Positivity in Managing Anxiety Disorders

Positive Self-Talk: Replace self-criticism with positive self-talk. Remind yourself of your capabilities and strengths when confronting fears.

If you're anxious about a job interview, use positive self-talk such as, "I have the skills and experience for this position."

Mindfulness and Relaxation: Practice mindfulness and relaxation techniques to calm the nervous system and reduce anxiety's physical symptoms.

When facing a stressful situation, engage in deep breathing exercises or mindfulness practices to manage your anxiety.

Seeking Professional Help When Needed

Therapy: Consider seeking help from a mental health professional, such as a therapist or counselor, to address anxiety disorders and phobias.

If your phobia significantly hinders your daily life and functioning, a therapist can provide specialized treatment options like exposure therapy or cognitive-behavioral therapy.

Medication: In some cases, medication prescribed by a psychiatrist may be beneficial in managing anxiety disorders. This should be done under professional guidance.

If you have a severe panic disorder, medication can be a valuable component of your treatment plan.

Turning Fear into an Opportunity for Personal Growth

Challenge and Growth: Confronting and conquering fears can lead to personal growth and increased self-confidence. View each challenge as an opportunity to learn and build resilience.

If you have a fear of water, learning to swim can be a transformative experience that boosts your confidence and opens up new recreational opportunities.

Embracing Change: Overcoming anxieties and phobias often involves embracing change. This willingness to face the unknown can lead to personal growth and a broader life perspective.

If you have a fear of change and uncertainty, taking on new experiences can lead to personal growth, adaptation, and an increased sense of self-efficacy.

Conquering anxieties and phobias is a profound journey of self-discovery and personal growth. By using strategies for confronting and overcoming fears, incorporating positivity into your anxiety management, seeking professional help when needed, and viewing fear as an opportunity for personal growth, you can emerge from the shadows of anxiety and phobias as a stronger, more resilient individual. These tips and real-life examples illustrate that fear can be a catalyst for personal transformation and a source of courage beyond what you ever thought possible.

Chapter 9: Harmony Within: The Mind-Body Connection

The mind and body are intricately linked, and the health of one profoundly influences the other. This chapter explores the profound connection between the mind and body, emphasizing the impact of positive thinking on physical health, techniques for reducing stress-related illnesses, the importance of mindful eating and exercise in promoting overall well-being, and the significance of embracing holistic wellness.

The Impact of Positive Thinking on Physical Health

Reduced Stress and Inflammation: Positive thinking has been associated with lower stress levels, which, in turn, can reduce inflammation in the body. Chronic inflammation is linked to various health conditions.

A positive outlook on life and effective stress management can contribute to lower inflammation levels, reducing the risk of inflammatory diseases.

Improved Immune Function: A positive mindset can enhance the immune system's ability to fight off infections and illnesses.

Research has shown that individuals who maintain a positive outlook are more likely to have stronger immune responses, increasing their resistance to diseases.

Techniques for Reducing Stress-Related Illnesses

Mindfulness and Meditation: Regular mindfulness practices, such as meditation, help reduce stress and its impact on the body. These practices encourage relaxation and mental clarity.

Incorporating a daily meditation routine can lead to decreased stress and improved overall health.

Progressive Muscle Relaxation: This technique involves systematically tensing and relaxing muscle groups to reduce physical tension and stress.

By practicing progressive muscle relaxation regularly, individuals can lower their risk of stress-related conditions like tension headaches and high blood pressure.

Mindful Eating and Exercise as Tools for Well-Being

Mindful Eating: Mindful eating encourages a deeper connection with your body and food. It promotes healthy eating habits and helps prevent overeating.

When practicing mindful eating, individuals savor each bite, listen to their body's hunger cues, and make healthier food choices, ultimately improving their overall well-being.

Regular Exercise: Physical activity releases endorphins, which are natural mood elevators. Exercise not only promotes physical health but also improves mental well-being.

Engaging in regular exercise routines, such as daily walks or workouts, can boost both physical and mental health, reducing the risk of depression and chronic diseases.

Embracing Holistic Wellness

Balanced Lifestyle: Holistic wellness encompasses the mind, body, and spirit. Maintaining a balanced lifestyle, including self-care practices, social connections, and relaxation, is vital for overall health.

Practicing holistic wellness can involve activities like yoga, spending time in nature, or engaging in hobbies that nurture the mind and spirit.

Connection with Nature: Spending time in nature has been linked to improved mental and physical health. Nature provides a sense of peace, rejuvenation, and connection.

Regular hikes, picnics, or nature walks can be a powerful tool for achieving holistic wellness, as they contribute to stress reduction and a sense of inner peace.

The mind-body connection is a fundamental aspect of overall well-being. By recognizing the impact of positive thinking on physical health, employing techniques for reducing stress-related illnesses, practicing mindful eating and regular exercise, and embracing holistic wellness, you can achieve a state of harmony within yourself. These tips and real-life examples illustrate that nurturing the mind-body connection not only enhances physical health but also promotes emotional and spiritual well-being, fostering a sense of wholeness and vitality.

Chapter 10: The Art of Positive Communication: Building Strong Relationships

Effective communication is the cornerstone of any successful relationship. This chapter explores the power of positive communication and offers tips for achieving it in various aspects of life. It emphasizes the importance of active listening and empathy, conflict resolution, negotiation from a positive perspective, and building trust and understanding in your interactions.

Effective Communication for Positive Relationships

Positive communication is essential for nurturing strong, healthy relationships. It involves the exchange of thoughts, ideas, and feelings with clarity and respect. Here are some tips for achieving effective communication:

Open and Honest Dialogue: Encourage open and honest discussions with your loved ones. Share your thoughts and feelings while also being receptive to theirs.

Clear Expression: Clearly express your thoughts and intentions. Avoid vague or confusing language that can lead to misunderstandings.

Non-Verbal Communication: Be mindful of your body language and facial expressions. Non-verbal cues can speak louder than words, so maintain a positive demeanor during conversations.

Active Engagement: Engage actively in conversations by asking questions, seeking clarification, and showing genuine interest in the other person's perspective.

Active Listening and Empathy

Active listening and empathy are integral components of positive communication. These skills foster understanding, trust, and stronger connections with others. To achieve them, consider the following tips:

Focused Attention: Give your full attention to the speaker. Avoid distractions and truly listen to what they are saying.

Empathetic Understanding: Try to understand the speaker's feelings and perspective. Put yourself in their shoes to empathize with their emotions.

Reflective Responses: Respond to the speaker by reflecting on what they've shared. Reiterate their main points and express your understanding.

Validation: Validate the speaker's emotions and experiences. Acknowledge their feelings, even if you don't agree with their viewpoint.

Conflict Resolution and Negotiation from a Positive Perspective

Conflict is a natural part of any relationship. However, how you approach and resolve conflicts can determine the health and longevity of your relationships. Here are tips for handling conflicts and negotiations with a positive perspective:

Maintain Respect: Regardless of the conflict's intensity, always maintain respect for the other person. Avoid personal attacks or insults.

Active Problem-Solving: Focus on finding solutions to the issue rather than dwelling on the problem itself. Collaborate with the other party to resolve the conflict.

Empowerment: Encourage a sense of empowerment in both parties involved. Ensure that everyone feels heard and valued during the conflict resolution process.

Compromise and Flexibility: Be willing to compromise and remain flexible. Sometimes, finding a middle ground is the best solution for both parties.

Positivity in Communication: Use positive language and tone during conflicts. Instead of saying, "You always do this," say, "I would appreciate it if we could find a solution together."

Building Trust and Understanding

Trust and understanding are the foundation of positive communication and strong relationships. To build and maintain these elements, consider the following tips:

Consistency: Be consistent in your words and actions. Trust is nurtured when others can rely on your promises and commitments.

Transparency: Be transparent and honest in your communication. Share your thoughts and feelings openly to foster understanding.

Accountability: Take responsibility for your actions and admit when you're wrong. Accountability is a vital component of trust and understanding.

Forgiveness: Be willing to forgive and move past conflicts. Holding onto grudges can erode trust and hinder understanding.

Mutual Respect: Always show respect for the other person's thoughts and feelings, even when you disagree. Respect is the cornerstone of trust and understanding.

Achieving Positive Communication in Practice

To achieve positive communication in practice, consider a real-life example. Imagine a couple, Sarah and Alex, who are experiencing a disagreement over household responsibilities. Sarah feels overwhelmed by her workload, while Alex believes he is doing his fair share.

Positive communication in this scenario would involve:

Open Dialogue: Sarah and Alex openly discuss their feelings and perceptions regarding household responsibilities. They maintain respect for each other's viewpoints.

Active Listening and Empathy: Sarah actively listens to Alex's perspective and empathizes with his point of view. She acknowledges that he feels he is contributing fairly.

Conflict Resolution: The couple collaborates to find a solution. They agree to a fair division of responsibilities and make a plan to implement it.

Building Trust and Understanding: Sarah and Alex commit to being transparent about their feelings and expectations moving forward. They acknowledge the importance of mutual respect and understanding in their relationship.

In conclusion, positive communication is the cornerstone of successful relationships. By employing effective communication techniques, active listening, empathy, constructive conflict resolution, and building trust and understanding, you can foster strong connections and mutual growth in all your interactions. These tips, illustrated through the example of Sarah and Alex, emphasize that positive communication is not only a tool for resolving conflicts but also a vehicle for nurturing lasting, harmonious relationships.

Chapter 11: Thriving Through Life's Storms: Resilience in Adversity

Resilience is the ability to bounce back and thrive in the face of adversity. This chapter delves into the power of maintaining a positive mindset in challenging times, turning setbacks into comebacks, the importance of learning from challenges and failures, and the significance of maintaining hope and optimism during tough times. These tips offer guidance on how to develop and enhance resilience in your life.

Thriving in the Face of Adversity with a Positive Mindset

A positive mindset is a crucial foundation for resilience. It can help you navigate life's storms with grace and determination. Here are some tips for maintaining a positive outlook:

Mindful Acceptance: Accept that adversity is a part of life, and difficult moments are inevitable. Mindful acceptance can reduce the emotional impact of challenges.

Focus on Solutions: When adversity strikes, concentrate on solutions rather than dwelling on the problem. This proactive approach can help you regain control.

Gratitude Practice: Cultivate a gratitude practice to remind yourself of the positive aspects of life, even during tough times. Gratitude can improve your mental well-being.

Positive Self-Talk: Use positive self-talk to counteract negative thoughts. Remind yourself of your strengths, capabilities, and past successes.

Turning Setbacks into Comebacks

Resilience involves turning setbacks into comebacks, using failures as stepping stones to success. Here are strategies to achieve this:

Adaptability: Embrace change and adapt to new circumstances. An adaptable approach allows you to recover and progress despite setbacks.

Set Realistic Goals: Set realistic and achievable goals. This ensures that your expectations align with your capabilities and the circumstances you face.

Perseverance: Keep moving forward, even when faced with challenges. Perseverance is a key trait of resilient individuals.

Seek Support: Don't be afraid to seek support from friends, family, or professionals when needed. They can provide guidance and encouragement during difficult times.

Learning from Challenges and Failures

Challenges and failures can be powerful teachers. Resilience involves learning from these experiences to grow stronger. Here's how to do it:

Self-Reflection: Engage in self-reflection to gain insight into the lessons learned from challenges and failures. This process can promote personal growth.

Adaptation and Improvement: Apply the knowledge gained from setbacks to adapt and improve. Use this new wisdom to navigate future challenges more effectively.

Embrace Change: Welcome change as an opportunity for growth and transformation. Change can lead to valuable insights and personal development.

Mental Flexibility: Cultivate mental flexibility by embracing different perspectives and new ways of thinking. A flexible mindset helps you overcome challenges with creativity.

Maintaining Hope and Optimism During Tough Times

Maintaining hope and optimism during tough times is a fundamental aspect of resilience. Here are strategies to stay positive:

Positive Visualization: Use positive visualization techniques to imagine successful outcomes. This can boost hope and motivation.

Cultivate Optimism: Cultivate an optimistic outlook by focusing on the positive aspects of situations, even when faced with adversity.

Self-Care: Prioritize self-care to maintain mental and emotional well-being. Activities such as exercise, relaxation, and mindfulness promote positivity.

Seek Inspiration: Surround yourself with sources of inspiration, such as books, people, or quotes that uplift your spirits and promote optimism.

Achieving Resilience in Practice

To illustrate achieving resilience in practice, consider an example of an individual facing a major setback in their career. Let's call this individual James.

James lost his job unexpectedly, and he was devastated. His resilience journey involved the following steps:

Positive Mindset: James began by accepting his situation mindfully. He acknowledged that job loss is a challenge that many people face at some point in their lives.

Turning Setbacks into Comebacks: Instead of succumbing to despair, James focused on solutions. He decided to update his skills and network with professionals in his industry.

Learning from Challenges and Failures: James reflected on the reasons for his job loss and identified areas for improvement. He used this insight to prepare for future interviews and job applications.

Maintaining Hope and Optimism: James visualized himself in a new, fulfilling job. He surrounded himself with positive influences and practiced self-care to stay motivated and optimistic.

In time, James secured a new position that he found even more fulfilling than his previous one. His journey of resilience and positive thinking allowed him to turn a setback into a successful comeback.

Therefore, resilience in adversity is a powerful tool for navigating life's challenges with grace and determination. By maintaining a positive mindset, turning setbacks into comebacks, learning from challenges and failures, and sustaining hope and optimism during tough times, you can build the strength to thrive through life's storms. These tips, exemplified by James's journey, illustrate that adversity can be a stepping stone to personal growth and ultimate success.

Chapter 12: Unbreakable Spirit: The Ultimate Resilience

The concluding chapter of "You Can't Hurt Me" encapsulates the ultimate resilience that can be achieved through a positive mindset. It invites you to reflect on your journey towards a positive life, celebrate your victories over negativity, empower yourself to face any challenge, and embrace the unshakable strength of a positive mindset. By weaving these insights and practical tips into your life, you can cultivate an unbreakable spirit that defies adversity and flourishes in the face of challenges.

Reflecting on Your Journey to a Positive Life

Reflecting on your journey is a pivotal step in understanding the growth and transformation you've experienced. It allows you to recognize how far you've come, the challenges you've overcome, and the resilience you've developed. To achieve this, consider the following tips:

Keep a Journal: Maintain a journal to document your experiences and emotions throughout your journey. This serves as a valuable tool for self-reflection.

Set Milestones: Establish milestones that mark your progress and achievements. Celebrate these milestones as a way of acknowledging your growth.

Self-Appreciation: Practice self-appreciation by acknowledging the effort you've invested in your personal development. Recognize the strength it took to overcome challenges and setbacks.

Gratitude: Express gratitude for the lessons you've learned, the people who have supported you, and the opportunities you've seized along the way.

Celebrating Your Victories Over Negativity

Victories over negativity are moments of triumph in your journey toward positivity. These victories can be small or significant, but they all contribute to your ultimate resilience. Here's how to celebrate them:

Acknowledge Your Strength: Acknowledge the strength and resilience you demonstrated in overcoming negativity and adversity.

Share Your Success: Share your success stories with others, inspiring them to embark on their journeys toward positivity and resilience.

Reward Yourself: Celebrate your victories with small rewards or treats as a way of recognizing your accomplishments.

Reflect on Lessons: Reflect on the lessons you've gained from your victories over negativity. These lessons can be applied to future challenges.

Empowering Yourself to Face Any Challenge

Empowerment is the key to facing any challenge with confidence and determination. To empower yourself, consider the following strategies:

Self-Belief: Cultivate a deep sense of self-belief. Recognize your abilities and potential to overcome challenges.

Problem-Solving Skills: Sharpen your problem-solving skills to tackle adversity head-on. Approach challenges with a proactive mindset.

Resilience Toolkit: Develop a personal resilience toolkit filled with strategies, techniques, and resources to navigate various challenges.

Support Network: Surround yourself with a support network of friends, family, or mentors who can offer guidance and encouragement.

Embracing the Unshakable Strength of a Positive Mindset

An unshakable strength lies within a positive mindset. It's a reservoir of determination and resilience that can weather any storm. To embrace the unshakable strength of a positive mindset, follow these guidelines:

Optimism: Maintain an optimistic outlook, seeing every challenge as an opportunity for growth.

Adaptability: Cultivate adaptability to navigate change and uncertainty with grace.

Self-Compassion: Practice self-compassion, treating yourself with kindness and understanding during challenging times.

Mindfulness: Engage in mindfulness practices to stay present and grounded, even when faced with adversity.

Positive Affirmations: Use positive affirmations to reinforce your belief in your abilities and resilience.

Visualize Success: Visualize success in the face of adversity, fostering a sense of empowerment and determination.

Achieving Unbreakable Spirit in Practice

To illustrate achieving an unbreakable spirit in practice, let's consider an example of an individual named Maya.

Maya faced several adversities in her life, including financial struggles, personal loss, and health challenges. However, her unbreakable spirit and positive mindset allowed her to navigate these challenges with resilience:

Reflecting on Her Journey: Maya kept a journal where she documented her challenges, setbacks, and achievements. Reflecting on her journey, she realized how her resilience had grown, even in the face of overwhelming adversity.

Celebrating Victories Over Negativity: Maya acknowledged her victories, no matter how small they may have seemed. Whether it was finding a temporary job during a tough financial period or regaining her health, she celebrated each success.

Empowering Herself: Maya believed in her ability to face any challenge. She sought financial advice to improve her financial situation, connected with a support network to cope with her personal loss, and worked with medical professionals to manage her health.

Embracing the Unshakable Strength of a Positive Mindset: Through it all, Maya maintained an optimistic outlook. She visualized herself overcoming each challenge and adapted to the uncertainties that came her way.

In the end, Maya's unbreakable spirit and positive mindset allowed her to not only survive adversity but thrive. She emerged from each challenge stronger, wiser, and more resilient.

In conclusion, the ultimate resilience achieved through a positive mindset is a testament to the strength of the human spirit. By reflecting on your journey, celebrating your victories over negativity, empowering yourself to face any challenge, and embracing the unshakable strength of a positive mindset, you can develop a spirit that is truly unbreakable. These tips, exemplified by Maya's journey, illustrate that with the right mindset and strategies, adversity can be transformed into an opportunity for personal growth, unwavering strength, and boundless potential.

Printed in Great Britain
by Amazon